THE TAO
of Modern Living

by Richard Combes
cover by Jim Lefevre

Nightingale

An imprint of Wimbledon Publishing Company
LONDON

Copyright © 2000
Illustrations © 2000 WPC

First published in Great Britain in 2000
by Wimbledon Publishing Company Ltd
P.O. Box 9779 London SW19 7ZG
All rights reserved

First published 2000 in Great Britain

ISBN: 1903222 17 6

Produced in Great Britain
Printed and bound in Hungary

2000 years of evolution have produced staggering advances in the civilisation of mankind. We have conquered space, split the atom and developed the technology to communicate across the globe at the touch of a button. On the downside there is the Shopping Channel.
But while space travel, split atoms and global communications are all very well, what good are they when you can't get the lid off a jar, pronounce the word 'falafel', or stop your hair from going all big? No good at all.

Long before the world even embarked on the first millennium, Taoist writers recognised that life is very much like a pig on a spacehopper - far beyond the comprehension or control of mortal man. They taught us that in the feast of life we must accept what is on our plate.

Yes, even genetically modified Brussels sprouts.

THE TAO

The Tao is that from which one cannot deviate; that from which one can deviate is not the Tao.

Or, put more simply:

Everything that is is the Tao and that that is not the Tao is not (the Tao).

Be wary of those who deny the feasibility of this central truth...

Such people lack the necessary spiritual depths. Such people sully the glorious sandals of summer with the socks of shame. Such people spend many hours noting the details of identical locomotives. Such people know more about Star Trek than is decent or legal. Such people clothe their dogs in tartan. Such people dance in lines.

Fear such people.

This difficult concept has been further explained as that that may be attained but never seen.

Think gross earnings.

YIN & YANG

Those who say that they would have right without its correlate, wrong, or good government without it's correlate, misrule, do not apprehend the great principles of the universe.

(Chuang-tzu)

The two central elements
are complements, not opposites.

Understanding of this concept comes
easiest of all to women during the
gestation period, for whom the bringing
together of tuna and Häagen-Dazs is
really no big deal.

A tale to best demonstrate this principle is that of the itinerant farmers who settled in a desolate clearing on the side of the mountain. Finding no building materials whatsoever they utilised the waste products from themselves and their animals to fashion humble dwellings.

Meditating in his hut one day, one of the farmers was suddenly struck with two fundamental truths: that in life from the endings come the beginnings; and, perhaps more importantly, that he really did need to make strenuous efforts to get out more. Either that or carve himself a window.

WU WEI

This most vital aspect of the Tao is the knowledge that there is little to be gained from attempting to fight the forces of nature. We must swim with the current, wobble with the jelly and jiggle with the tassels.

It is only the foolish man who tries
to swim against the current.
The man whose car is so big the
licensing authority has to classify it
under 'military vehicles'.
The man whose gates are tastefully
adorned with his own initials.
The man who lives by the creed,
'If it's good for golf,
it's good for casual'.

You know the man. He's foolish.

The laws of nature operate every day to
show why resistance is futile. Allow
yourself to be swept along with the
other floaters and enjoy the ride.

The greatest perfection seems imperfect.
(Lao-tzu)

THE MIRRORS OF DECEPTION

An item of clothing may seem to complement you in every possible way in the shop. Once you try the same garment on at home you will discover that you actually resemble someone who has recently escaped from a secure unit for clowns.

THE LOCKS OF DISTRESS.

Once the hairdresser has finished his task, he will inevitably share the wonders with you by raising a mirror behind your head and asking your opinion. To your dismay the reflection will show a turnip that has been battered beyond recognition by a machete. Your indignation and rage is best expressed with the words, "Lovely, how much do I owe you?".

You must go neither too slowly nor too fast. (Chuang-tzu)

THE LANES OF FURY

Upon moving your vehicle to a different lane in order to speed your progress you will notice two things. Your new lane is moving slower than the tectonic plates. Your old lane now resembles a multiple entry land speed record bid.

THE ETERNAL CYCLE

Your recently purchased, astronomically expensive mountain bike is designed to allow you to glide effortlessly up some of the most extreme gradients found in the wilds of nature.

Hold this thought as, with the veins on your forehead standing out like uncooked sausages, you labour up a slight incline on the way to the shops.

The greatest dexterity seems awkward.
(Lao-tzu)

THE DANCE OF THE FOOLISH

At any social gathering involving communal dancing, excess intoxicants will allow you to move with a natural sensation of rhythm and poise. The gift of sight will allow onlookers to witness the only roller skating baboon in captivity.

THE HOP OF HOPE

Only attempt to change a garment using a towel to cover your modesty if you are sure that you have the energy to hop for up to half a mile across jagged pebbles. In front of an audience.

You have had the nerve to be born human, and you are delighted.
(Chuang-tzu)

THE PILES OF SORROW.

When visiting a chemist to collect a prescription for a particularly sensitive problem share the sensation of communal healing with those present in the shop as the counter assistant shouts your order through to the back. Twice.

THE WEB OF DECEIT

You are delighted that your boss shows a keen personal interest in the development of your work. Sadly you struggle to explain how downloading the 'Thai Me Up, Thai Me Down' website is an essential part of your research.

Not to know is the beginning of truth, pretending to know can be an obstacle.
(Lao-tzu)

THE STICKS OF ANGER

In a Chinese restaurant impress your dining companions by greeting the chopsticks like old friends. Their admiration will grow as noodles are twirled like lassos and prawn balls sent rolling to the far corners of the table. Enjoy that special moment as the waitress finally presents you with the fork of frustration.

THE SECRET NAME

Microseconds after being introduced to someone at a party you will notice that you couldn't remember their name even if a harpoon was trained on your genitalia. Compound your folly by introducing them to a third party with the words, "Have you met this crazy guy?" and silently letting yourself out through a back door.

The greatest eloquence seems stammering

(Lao-tzu)

THE BREATH OF SURPRISE

Chance encounters with members of the opposite sex you are keen to impress will most likely occur shortly after the feast of the salami and spring onion torpedo.

THE ETERNAL QUESTION

There can be nothing more beautiful or rewarding than the moment when your child speaks it's first words. Until they learn the word, "why?". Now you must repeat the mantra, "Because it just bloody is, OK?".

He is as cold as autumn, and warm as spring, for his joy and anger occur as naturally as the four seasons.
(Chuang-tzu)

THE SHORTS OF SORROW
On the first warm, sunny day of the year, leave the house resplendent in your newest and most garish beachwear. Return later gripped by the first throws of pneumonia having been caught in an arctic shower.
Changeable, isn't it?

THE SHOWER OF CONFUSION

Using the shower in your flat served by communal plumbing will allow you to contemplate the paradox of the yin/yang polarity, thanks largely to the constant switch from jets of white nuclear heat on the one hand, to shards of the purest Siberian rain water on the other.
Chant as you do so.

For learning well there is nothing better than moderation.

THE WANDERING SAGE

On any form of public transport look out for this bedraggled, aromatic, hirsute man of wisdom. You can be sure that it will be you that he will choose to impart his thoughts to. Drink from the fountain of his knowledge but not from his bottle of pine varnish.

THE GREAT MIX OF LIFE

At some unspecified stage of your adolescent development you will inevitably be made aware of one of the most central truths of existence. Malibu and scrumpy do not mix.

The best will in the world, when forced, achieves nothing. (Lao-tzu)

GATHERING FOR THE LIGHTING OF COALS IN THE SUMMER MONTHS TO HASTEN RAIN

When hosting a barbecue, always remember that an unidentifiable piece of carrion torched to hell and back on the outside, whilst still bloody and twitching within is a wonderful gift to be treasured and savoured but, under no circumstances, eaten.

THE ETERNAL SCREAM

The serene face of a tiny baby is a picture of wonder and joy bringing tranquillity and harmony to all who see it. Until you try and amuse one with some funny faces. Now that same face will register confusion, dismay, dislike, disgust and scream so loudly that everyone within a three-mile radius turns and gives you a dirty look.

There must be co-ordination of mind and hand. Words cannot explain what it is but there is some mysterious art herein. (Chuang-tzu)

THE WAVES OF DESPAIR

Impress your dinner guest by suavely summoning the waiter with a debonair wave of the hand. When your fifth attempt to catch his eye fails you will notice that you suddenly possess all the charm and sophistication of a half-eaten pickled egg discarded in an ashtray.

THE SHAKE OF FEAR

As you emerge from a WC with inadequate hand-drying facilities a colleague or acquaintance will magically appear. During the following handshake they will eye you with suspicion and, with any luck, disgust.

Let the ear hear what it longs to hear. (Lieh-tzu)

THE AGONY OF YOUTH

Shortly after setting out on a journey of any length on foot or by car your children will be instantly transformed into medical wonders by complaining of ailments as yet unknown to science. "My hair's sore", "My teeth itch", "I've sprained my lip".

Let the eye see what it wants to see. (Lieh-tzu)

THE CORE IS HARD

Suggesting a visit to an art-house movie to your date will demonstrate your diverse cultural interests. Now demonstrate your ability to slide down into your seat quietly weeping, as your chosen movie turns out to be the most filthy animal-based porn extravaganza this side of Amsterdam.

TE
THE POWER WITHIN

Now that you have learnt the importance of going with the flow, utilise this knowledge to release your inner power. This is the power found in the ancient fighting arts of judo and aikido where the opponent is defeated with the force of his own attack. In this way many opponents will seem to be thrown to the floor without actually being touched.

Those of you familiar with Italian football will already know this one.

The superior man goes through his life without any one preconceived course of action or any taboo... The goody-goodies are the thieves of virtue. (Chuang-tzu)

Beware such goody-goodies.
They were the ones who, in primary music class, didn't find it amusing that all the recorders smelt of sick, and, no, didn't want to have a sniff. They are the ones who meet their targets and won't clock you out. They will be the ones who wear brown leather gloves to drive, kneel on a little prayer mat to garden and drag a caravan with them wheresoever they may go.

You know the ones.

Tranquility in disturbance means perfection. (Chuang-tzu)

PRIORITISE YOUR ENERGIES

When dining with friends demonstrate your appreciation for their hospitality by responding to any attempt to engage you in conversation with the palm of disinterest whilst your free hand shovels away the food in a bestial fashion.

THE ART OF FENG SHUI

For the optimum positive results place a large plank horizontally across the door. Position the couch three feet from the television screen and balance the symmetry of the line on the one side with a bucket of fried chicken and, on other with a bar of chocolate the size of a headstone.

The best employer of men keeps himself below them. (Lao-tzu)

THE CLEANSING OF FALSEHOOD

At the conclusion of a job interview when asked if there is anything you would like to know about the company enquire as to their gullibility when it comes to swallowing sick-leave stories.

SPEAK ONLY THE TRUTH

Should your employer discover you sprawled in the recovery position semi-comatose across your desk of a Friday afternoon and offer the somewhat insincere enquiry, 'Busy?", maintain the karmic positivity with an honest, "Well obviously not, cretin."

SEEK NEW LIMITS

No excuse for late arrival at your place of work is complete without a reference to capture by and escape from winged sea monkeys.

THE SLEEP OF THE JUST

Should your boss spot you slipping a pillow into your office after lunch, insist that it's just a pile cushion.

*The best soldier is not soldierly,
the best fighter is not ferocious.*
(Lao-tzu)

SHARE THE GIFT OF DOWNWARD MOBILITY

When a mobile phone user disrupts your bus journey by shouting that they are 'on the bus', appropriate the phone, hurl them from the still moving vehicle and update the party on the other end by pointing out that they are now 'in the gutter'.

THE THREE STRIKE RULE

If anyone explains the fact that that they cannot assist you in some way by stating that "it's more than my job's worth", strike them three times. Few people realise that this is actually permitted by law.

By letting the emotions follow as they will, you avoid fatigue.

(Chuang-tzu)

STUDIOUS INACTION

An armchair provides the ideal setting for quiet contemplation and wonder at the myriad of beautiful delights that are to be found in creation. Such as televised sports.

THE TALE OF WOE

When cornered during a social gathering by a man you recognise as the Storyteller of Tedium, who has opened with, 'A funny thing happened to a chap I once knew," immediately insert, 'Really? Well I never. What a great story." Run like a hare in the confusion.

What the mind wants is liberty to stray whither it will, and if it has not this freedom, the very nature of man is cramped and thwarted. (Chuang-tzu)

LOOK TO THE FUTURE

Ambition is an essential ingredient of a healthy psyche, allowing us to glimpse brave new worlds and reach for the stars. Make a start tomorrow.
Or the day after.

INTELLECTUAL EXERCISE

A civilised and adult exchange of views can ease tension and clear the air. Alternatively you can simply respond to everything the other party says by sing-songing, "whoo-a-ooh" at them in a primary school playground manner. You'll never lose.

The capacity of the mind is broad and huge, like the vast sky.
(Tan-Ching)

THE REMOTENESS OF THOUGHT

As the most vital organ in the development of the self, the brain should be constantly fed with new and varied stimuli. Change channel as often as you can be bothered.

THE DECEIT OF FRIENDS

Any product description coining the phrase 'user-friendly' must be treated with a mine of salt. A higher level of contentment will be achieved by sticking to those products marked, 'lobotomised imbecile proof'.

Learn by being, work without strain.
(Lao-tzu)

THE TAO OF TEA

In the event of a mechanical failure to your car, pop up the bonnet, take a couple of steps back, suck in your breath and shake your head sadly whilst muttering, "Oh dear, oh dear, oh dear, oh dear." Go and put the kettle on. You have now completed 85% of the 'labour' needed on the vehicle.

THE LANGUAGE OF THE DAMNED

When an overly ambitious colleague enquires about your progress, terrify them by explaining that you are currently trying to arrange to 'pull some of the big guns in for a round-table bounce around session with the ultimate aim of hitting the ground running'. They depart to have nightmares, you return to your office to finish those doughnuts prior to your afternoon nap.

Let the body have every comfort that it craves. (Lieh-tzu)

BALANCE IS ESSENTIAL IN ALL ASPECTS OF LIFE

If you find yourself losing yours you can bet that that fourteenth pint was a bit off. Or maybe you ate something.

THE FEAST OF THE DAWN

When we rise for a new day our bodies are an empty shell into which much goodness must flow. If it doesn't include a loaf of fried bread and a string of battered saveloys, it doesn't count.

> When a man has perfect virtue (Te), fire cannot burn him, water cannot drown him, cold and heat cannot afflict him, birds and beasts cannot injure him. (Lao-tzu)

THE WONDER OF NEW LIFE

Remark to a follically challenged new father, "well, he's certainly got your hair". If you know him to be sensitive on this point, you may clap him heartily on the back as you say it.

WALK WITH THE ANIMALS

To truly be at one with nature's creatures when walking in a park or public place, find a dogwalker. Leap on them, lick them, claw at them and feel perfectly free to nuzzle their groin. Respond to any complaint with a cheery, "It's all right, I'm only playing".

When knowledge and cleverness arrived there came great deceptions. (Lao-tzu)

THE PATTER OF TINY BRAIN CELLS

When a salesman assures you that a particular model is indispensable as it is fitted with a G49 double reactor loop, tap your index finger gently against your forehead as you explain that this particular model is fitted with a brain and that if he doesn't cut the crap you will smite him dead with a half brick.

THE MUSIC OF THE AGES

The true pathway to wisdom is through the passage of the generations. Bless the young and foolish with the mantra of the ages, "All music sounds the same these days, you can't hear what they're saying, they don't play proper instruments any more...And it's too loud."

Fear is a great illusion. (Lao-tzu)

THE SOOTHING JEST

When called unexpectedly to see your boss discard worthless feelings of trepidation and supplant them with an aura of equality. "Come on then, tubby, what's on your mind?" may be a worthy opening gambit, as you apply a playful headlock.

THE COVERING OF NAKEDNESS

In a situation that requires you to address a large number of your colleagues or peers calm yourself by imagining them all naked. Now calm yourself further by dressing the men as The Village People and the women as extras from *Spacevixens*.

True wisdom seems foolish. True art seems artless. (Lao-tzu)

ART ENLIVENS THE SENSES

Visit a gallery of modern art. Stand with arms folded, stroking your chin and staring studiously at the fire extinguisher muttering, "Mmm, it's bold yet understated". Or words to that effect.

THE BLUFF OF DELIGHT

When faced with a pseudo intellectual culture snob test their stupidity with tales of some recent events that you have enjoyed. "I think Puccini can only be done properly underwater, and as for that new version of Hamlet, well, the stilts do lend it a certain gravitas, don't you think?"

Be content with your world, celebrate the way things are.
(Lao-tzu)

THE FINAL WORD

It is only the extraordinarily foolish man who moans about today and worries about tomorrow. The man who understands that we are all prawns in the great chess game of life is indeed wise. If a little confused.